The Toll-house of Suffolk

Patrick Taylor

POLYSTAR PRESS

ISBN 978 1 907154 00 3

The Toll-houses of Suffolk

Published by
Polystar Press
277 Cavendish Street
Ipswich Suffolk IP3 8BQ
(01473) 434604
polystar@ntlworld.com

ISBN 978 1 907154 00 3

Typeset by nattygrafix

Printed by
R Booth
The Praze, Penryn

Contents

Illustrations

In Memory of Doreen

'without whose daughter'

0.0 Introduction

As long ago as 1978, when I was fresh out of architectural school and living in Cornwall, it was resolved that toll-houses would be a worthwhile subject for further study - "one day" was the term used at the time I believe.

Years passed, life was got on with, and it was not until 1992 as a Cornishman abroad in Suffolk, that I went to study for an MA in Conservation Studies at the University of York. Here I encountered the phenomenon of local distinctiveness and realised that the toll-houses, built for the most part during the early industrial revolution before the coming of the railways, might be a good indicator. My dissertation in 1995 followed this hunch through and included as part of my study of local distinctiveness, a comparison between the toll-houses in the two counties I knew best, Cornwall and Suffolk.

This book and its companion volume 'The Toll-houses of Cornwall' draw heavily on that dissertation, consisting mainly of extracts relevant to each county, together with new gazetteer sections based on my research for the dissertation. My thanks must therefore go to my tutors at York, Professor John Worthington and Peter Burman, and to the staff at Suffolk Record Office for their assistance with my research and illustrations.

Although they did not go forward with this book, I must also thank the Suffolk Institute of Archaeology and History for seriously considering this for publication. In the end, renewed impetus has come from the south-west with the recent publication of a joint effort with Tim Jenkinson on 'The Toll-houses of South Devon'. With this further companion volume we now anticipate a series, with North Devon and Norfolk planned for publication next year.

Finally, the dedication which goes to Pauline's mother, Doreen Tricker, a Sunderland girl who settled in Suffolk. She saw the beginnings of this book, but is sadly no longer with us to see the result.

Local Brick Toll-house,
Trumpington, Cambridge
photo: polystar

1

1.0 The Turnpike Roads

Mending the Highways
(from Smith - 1970)

CAP. VIII.
The ftatute for mending of highways.

FOR *amending of highways, being now both very noifom and tedious to travel in, and dangerous to all paffengers and carriages :*

(2) Be it enacted by the authority of this prefent parliament, that the conftables and church-wardens of every parifh within this realm, fhall yearly upon the *Tuefday* or *Wednefday* in *Eafter* week call together a number of the parifhioners, and fhall then elect and chufe two honeft perfons of the parifh to be furveyors and orderers for one year, or the works for amendment of the highways in their parifh leading to any market-town ; (3) the which perfons fhall have authority by virtue hereof, to order and direct the perfons and carriages that fhall be appointed for thofe works, by their difcretions ; (4) and the faid perfons fo named fhall take upon them the execution of their faid offices, upon pain every of them making default, to forfeit twenty fhillings.

(margin: Who fhall be charged towards the mending of highways. Surveyors fhall be appointed for the amendment of highways. 3 Mod. 96. 22Car.2.c.12. f. 12.)

II. And the faid conftables and church-wardens fhall then alfo name and appoint four days for the amending of the faid ways, before the feaft of the nativity of Saint *John Baptift* then next following ; (2) and fhall openly in the church the next *Sunday* after *Eafter* give knowledge of the fame four days ; (3) and upon the faid days the parifhioners fhall endeavour themfelves to the amending of the faid ways ; (4) and fhall be chargeable thereunto as followeth ; that is to fay, every perfon for every plow-land in tillage or pafture that he or fhe fhall occupy in the fame parifh, and every other perfon keeping there a draught or plough, fhall find and fend at every day and place to be appointed for the amending of the ways in that parifh as is aforefaid, one wain or cart furnifhed after the cuftom of the country with oxen, horfes or other cattle, and all other neceffaries meet to carry things convenient for that purpofe, and alfo two able men with the fame, upon pain of every draught making default, ten fhillings ; (5) and every other houfholder, and alfo every cottager and labourer of that parifh, able to labour, and being no hired fervant by the year, fhall by themfelves or one fufficient labourer for every of them, upon every of the faid four days, work and travel in the amendment of the faid highways, upon every of the faid four days, work and travel in the amendment of the faid highways, upon pain of every perfon making default, to lofe for every day twelve pence. (6) And if the faid carriages of the parifh, or any of them, fhall not be thought needful by the fupervifors to be occupied upon any of the faid days, that then every fuch perfon that fhould have fent any fuch carriage, fhall fend to the faid work for every carriage fo fpared two able men, there to labour for that day, upon pain to lofe for every man fo fent to the faid work, twelve pence. (7) And every perfon and carriage abovefaid fhall have and bring with them fuch fhovels, fpades, picks, mattocks,

(margin: Four days fhall be appointed for the amendment of highways. Six days are appointed by 5El.c.13.f.7. Each perfon's charge towards the mending of highways. Explained by 18 El. c. 10; f. 2. Neceffary tools fhall be brought to be)

Statute for Mending of Highways, 1555
(from Serjeant & Penrose - 1973)

3

1.1 The King's Highway

In order to understand the turnpike road system that gave rise to toll-houses in the eighteenth century we need first to look at its origins in the mists of medieval time.

Early roads were not actual parcels of real estate set aside for the purpose of transit as have evolved today, but rather lines of least resistance where a 'right of passage' existed - the King's Highway - over ground that remained in private ownership. This still exists in vestigial form in our modern footpath network, which then as now consisted of three levels of usage: footpaths, bridleways and carriageways (now roads used as public paths). In those days diversions were implemented to maintain the right of the traveller if the road was 'founderous' or his way was blocked, rather than at the request of the owner to suit the management of the land as is now often the case.

The highway was thus a 'communal property right' available freely for the use of any subject of the Crown and as such received little or no maintenance other than out of selfish necessity to overcome a particular obstacle such as a flood or fallen tree. It was therefore in no individual's interest to invest time or money in repairing something that would mainly benefit others.

As a consequence the roads were generally in a very poor state and greatly abused by heavy loads with many horses, by spiked or narrow wheels and by the dragging of sledges or timber. Similar problems exist to this day where the selfish interest of highway users will require legislation to achieve a benefit for the common good (e.g. the limitation of motor car use), and it was indeed legislation then that was a first step on the way to improvement of the situation. A parallel can be seen here with another communal property right, that of the old strip field system with attendant grazing and hunting rights, which was also abused by selfish interest and eventually put to rights by the legislation of the Enclosure Acts.

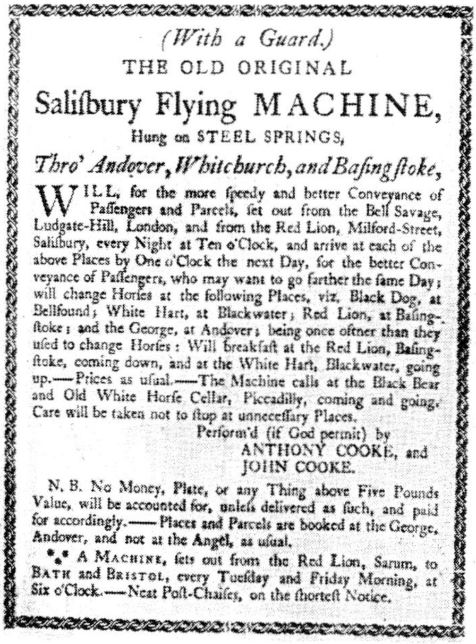

(With a Guard.)

THE OLD ORIGINAL

Salisbury Flying MACHINE,

Hung on STEEL SPRINGS,

Thro' Andover, Whitchurch, and Basingstoke,

WILL, for the more speedy and better Conveyance of Passengers and Parcels, set out from the Bell Savage, Ludgate-Hill, London, and from the Red Lion, Milford-Street, Salisbury, every Night at Ten o'Clock, and arrive at each of the above Places by One o'Clock the next Day, for the better Conveyance of Passengers, who may want to go farther the same Day; will change Horses at the following Places, viz. Black Dog, at Bellfound; White Hart, at Blackwater; Red Lion, at Basingstoke; and the George, at Andover; being once oftner than they used to change Horses: Will breakfast at the Red Lion, Basingstoke, coming down, and at the White Hart, Blackwater, going up.—Prices as usual.—The Machine calls at the Black Bear and Old White Horse Cellar, Piccadilly, coming and going. Care will be taken not to stop at unnecessary Places.

Perform'd (if God permit) by
ANTHONY COOKE, and
JOHN COOKE.

N. B. No Money, Plate, or any Thing above Five Pounds Value, will be accounted for, unless delivered as such, and paid for accordingly.—Places and Parcels are booked at the George, Andover, and not at the Angel, as usual.

₊ A MACHINE, sets out from the Red Lion, Sarum, to BATH and BRISTOL, every Tuesday and Friday Morning, at Six o'Clock.—Neat Post-Chaises, on the shortest Notice.

Salisbury Coach Service Poster
(from Wright - 1992)

1.2 Parish Responsibility

In the mid sixteenth century the state of the roads became of such concern that legislation was passed to firmly place the responsibility for their repair in the hands of the parish in which they were situated. The initial Act of 1555, in the brief reign of Mary Tudor, was a temporary measure which required each parish to elect two Surveyors. Their duty was to oversee the repair of roads by the inhabitants of that parish on four days per year when they were to provide 'statute labour'.

The larger landowners were also required to provide two men plus carts and tools whilst the Surveyors were permitted to dig for gravel on any waste land or commons adjoining the road. A further Act of 1562 extended the statute duties to six days per year and defaulters were liable to heavy fines.

Parishes that failed to maintain their roads properly were liable to be presented by the Justices to Quarter Sessions. If they then still failed to repair the roads satisfactorily they would be subject to indictment and the imposition of fines and/or additional days of statute labour. An occasional alternative to this was the raising of a Highway Rate by the Justices, which would then be used to pay for the necessary labour.

The problem which this system failed to tackle was that of the polluter not paying - the major users of the roads in a parish were not the inhabitants, but rather those passing through often with heavy loads for markets in other places. Their contribution to the effort of repair was made in their own parish and was but a fraction in recompense for the wear and tear they inflicted on the roads in general. The problem of selfish interest therefore remained during a period of increasing trade in the seventeenth century and was not helped by the unwillingness of labourers (one volunteer being worth ten pressed men) nor by Surveyors whose unpaid posts were held on an annual basis and led to low levels of skill and little continuity of effort.

14th Century Bridge,
Toppesfield, Hadleigh, Suffolk
photo: polystar

1.3 Available Technology

At the end of the seventeenth century in archaeological terms, the Iron Age was still very much in progress with timber, fired clay, stone and metal being the major materials for any significant undertaking. Power was sourced from either muscle, wind or water, all three being used in the various forms of mills at fixed locations, the former two for locomotion on land or water. The wonders of steam that could turn heat into motion were as yet unheard of and the nation's wealth was traded and defended by sailing ships of timber, tar and hemp rope.

The transportation of goods thus involved considerable effort and consequently costs away from the cheapest place of production rose sharply. A number of rivers had been made navigable but significant areas remained beyond the reach of water-borne transport. The roads thus acted as both feeders to the river system and as the main means of transport where the rivers did not reach. In addition some goods did not travel well by water, others might not risk military intervention at sea whilst even more were better walking themselves to market. Whilst road transport was many times more expensive per ton per mile, the differential being relatively less for more expensive goods, it was often the preferred alternative.

There was a large network of 'carriers' operating around the country, usually based at various inns and for the most part employing packhorses. The seventeenth century saw these augmented by increasing amounts of wheeled transport, largely as a result of the increasing size and quantity of goods being traded, which led ultimately to a renewed crisis on the roads. A response to this were the various 'Wheel Acts' which sought to limit the damage to the roads by legislating about permissible loads and wheel widths. These were doomed to failure as essentially against the spirit of the times they tried to contain the damage with preventative measures.

And Whereas the Wheels of many Carts, Carrs, and Brewers Drays, now commonly used for the Carriage of Goods, Beer, Ale, and other things, from place to place within the Cities of London and Westminster, and Parishes aforesaid, where the Streets are Paved, are made thinner or narrower in the Felleys then formerly, and many are Shod with Iron Tyres, by means whereof the Pavements in the Streets of the said Cities and Places are daily impaired and broken up, and made dirty and rough: For prevention whereof for the time to come, Be it therefore Enacted by the Authority aforesaid, That from and after the fifteenth day of December, the Wheels of every Cart, Carr or Dray to be used for the Carriage of any thing whatsoever, from any place within the said Cities and Places, to any place situate in the said Cities and Places where the Streets are Paved, shall be made to contain the full breadth of Six Inches in the Felley, and shall not be wrought about with any Iron Work whatsoever, nor be drawn with above the number of two horses, after they are up the hills from the Water-side; And the Owners and Pro-

Extract from London Wheel Act, 1690
(from Searle - 1930)

1.4 Justice Trusts

The parish repair system had taken each parish's previous Common Law obligation to maintain local roads and enshrined it in national legislation which was not in fact abolished until the General Highway Act of 1835. The system contained no requirement for the improvement of roads to cater for increased usage and was essentially an evenly applied remedy to a very uneven problem. Considerable differences existed between parishes both in terms of size and the numbers of roads to repair, population density and availability of labour and local geology which affected both the quality of substrate and availability of materials for repair. A further overlay of differing amounts of road usage near towns as trade increased and carriers turned to waggons and coaches led to a result that included many extremes.

In some parishes the roads were doubtless adequate whilst in others they were difficult to start with, poorly repaired and subject to increasingly heavy usage. This final straw was the key to a solution, the earliest tolls levied to pay for repair being those charged by the Justice trusts of the late seventeenth century. The first of these dates from 1663 and was set up to remedy problems on part of the Great North Road, where the Justices had previously tried all else at their disposal without success.

The concept of tolls was not new and had in the past been used to fund both 'pavage' and 'pontage' as well as to recoup costs for occasional private roads. Tolls had also been levied for markets, giving rise to a different type of toll-house in medieval times (see page 63). It was therefore no great leap to apply such a toll to remedy a problem on a particular public road, the Justices retaining control of both the tolled road and the others within a parish.

A further twelve Justice trusts were set up on particularly bad roads between 1696 and 1714 by which time the turnpike trust proper was beginning to emerge as a more suitable vehicle for setting the roads to rights.

15th Century Packhorse Bridge, Moulton, Suffolk
photo: polystar

1.5 Turnpike Trusts

The earliest turnpike trusts date from 1707 and, although still under the control of the Justices who were usually included amongst their number anyway, were run by trustees who were able to spread the administrative load of managing the roads which was threatening to swamp the Justices' other duties. The trusts were composed for the most part of local gentlemen and landowners, who as trustees were not able to profit from the trust itself. They could however foresee the relief afforded to their parishes by the indirect benefits of improved local economies that would ensue from making outsiders pay for the maintenance of the local roads.

Turnpike trusts were but one of many types of local 'ad hoc' body set up during the eighteenth century amongst which are included the Incorporated Guardians of the Poor. These latter set up 'Unions' of several parishes to build a workhouse, which could then be let as a going concern to a local manufacturer who would feed the occupants in return for the use of their labour, thus relieving the parishes of the burden of the poor. These were as much forerunners of local authority Social Services departments as the turnpike trusts were of Highways departments, both marking the beginnings of bringing various systems into public control, without incurring great expense.

It should be remembered that the turnpike trusts were no more than non profit making trusts set up to manage existing routes, very unlike the later canal and railway concerns which were joint stock companies with shareholders whose aim was to create new routes and make money. Each turnpike trust was set up by an Act of Parliament, usually following vigorous petitioning by local worthies about the state of the roads. Parliamentary permission was necessary because the enterprise required the extinction of the former communal right of free passage and it became usual for Acts to last for a period of twenty one years, although renewal was usually forthcoming.

Anno XV.

Caroli II. Regis.

An Act for Repairing
the High-ways within the Counties of *Hertford*, *Cambridge* and *Huntington*.

Whereas the ancient High-way and Post-Road leading from London to York, and so into Scotland, and likewise from London into Lincolnshire, lieth for many miles in the Counties of Hertford, Cambridge and Huntington, in many of which places the Road, by reason of the great and many Loads which are weekly drawn in Waggons through the said places, as well by reason of the great Trade of Barley and Mault that cometh

Extract from First Turnpike Act, 1663
(from Searle - 1930)

1.6 Turnpike Mania

In the years up to 1750 some 133 turnpike trusts received their Acts of Parliament and roads were turnpiked in two main areas. Firstly, and mainly before 1720, the network of radial roads emanating from London were covered by a number of linear trusts, each one's territory abutting the next.

This process continued in the following thirty years alongside the second concentration of town-centred trusts which developed along the Severn valley between Bristol (at that time England's second largest city) and a rapidly developing Birmingham. Around mid-century the turnpike idea seems to have captured the imagination in a big way and between 1751 and 1772 a further 418 Acts were passed, which effectively allowed the turnpike system to cover the country.

The uncertainties that led up to the American War of Independence brought this age of confidence to a sudden halt in 1773 and the ensuing years that also included the Napoleonic Wars saw greatly reduced activity in terms of new trusts. A further 400 or so trusts were set up between 1773 and 1836 of which 59 alone were in the years 1824 to 1826.

These later years of lesser activity were due in part to a saturation point being reached but should also be seen against the beginnings of the years of the boom in canal building from 1770 along with the industrial revolution getting into full swing, doubtless helped along its way by the greatly improved transport, trade and communications links provided by the turnpikes. The final mini-boom in turnpike activity of 1824 to 1826, probably represents a mopping up of the last remaining suitable routes in slightly improved times. Whilst Acts continued to be renewed throughout most of the nineteenth century, the last new Act of 1836 foreshadows the coming of the railways in the 1840's and the growing realisation that the days of the turnpikes were numbered.

'Gothick' Windows, Sicklesmere
(*Sudbury - Bury St Edmunds*)
photo: polystar

9

Toll-house Sale Poster, 1872
(from Serjeant & Penrose - 1973)

1.7 Winding Up

By the 1840's the turnpike road system had reached its greatest extent with over 20,000 miles of road under the control of over a thousand trusts. During the preceding century the growth and improvement of the system had greatly reduced travelling times and consequently enlarged the market place. Road construction techniques had gradually improved from the early days of simply piling another layer of gravel on top to the latter years, under the influence of great engineers like Telford or McAdam, when roads were rebuilt with a firm foundation and progressively smaller sized stones rolled in, to provide a freely draining cambered finish.

Inland transportation as a whole, with the complementary system of canals, had been greatly improved but not revolutionised, as it was still essentially bound by the limitations of muscle and wind power. It was the magic of steam in the form of the railways which ultimately brought the revolution. The turnpike system suffered first followed by the canals, as both were swept away as passengers and then freight took to the rails.

The turnpike trusts were thus subjected to falling receipts through the mid-nineteenth century which made it increasingly difficult for them to deliver the goods.

Lack of repairs led to a growing resentment to their charges amongst their customers, perhaps most strongly felt in Wales where the 'Rebecca' Riots of the 1840's saw the destruction of many gates and toll-houses by men disguised in female clothing, in imitation of the biblical Rebecca and her daughters.

By the 1870's the trusts were being wound up, their assets in the form of toll-houses and equipment were sold off, and the responsibility for the roads, which they still did not own, vested in the Highway Boards, forerunners of the County Councils.

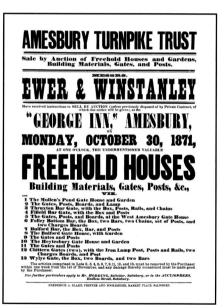

Toll-house Sale Poster, 1871
(from Wright - 1992)

2.0 Collecting the Tolls

Toll Gate Collection
(from Smith - 1970)

A TABLE of the TOLLS payable at this TURNPIKE GATE.
[By the Local Act.]

s d

FOR every Horse,Mule,Afs,or other Beast (Except Dogs) drawing
any Coach,Berlin,Landau,Barouche,Chariot,Chaise,Chair,Hearse,
Gig,Curricle,Whiskey,Taxed Cart,Waggon,Wain,Timber frame,Cart frame
Dray or other Vehicle of whatsoever description when drawn by more
than one Horse or other Beast the Sum of Four pence half-penny
Such Waggon,Wain,Cart,or other such Carriage having Wheels of
lefs breadth than four and a half inches _____ **$4\tfrac{1}{2}$**

AND when drawn by one Horse or other Beast only the sum of six pence
(Waggons,Wains and other such Carriages having Wheels as aforesaid) **6**

FOR every Dog drawing any Truck,Barrow or other Carriage for the
space of One Hundred Yards or upwards upon any part of the
said Roads, the Sum of One Penny _____ **1**

FOR every Horse,Mule,Afs,or other Beast laden or unladen and
not drawing, the Sum of Two-pence _____ **2**

FOR every carriage moved or propelled by Steam or Machinery or
by any other power than Animal power the Sum of one Shilling for
each Wheel thereof _____ **1 0**

FOR every Score of Oxen,Cows or neat Cattle, the Sum of Ten-pence
and so in Proportion for any greater or lefs Number _____ **10**

FOR every Score of Calves,Sheep,Lambs or Swine the Sum of Five
pence and so in proportion for any greater or lefs Number _____ **5**

(By 4.G.4.C.95)

FOR every Horse,Mule,Afs or other Beast drawing any Waggon
Wain,Cart or other such Carriage having the Fellies of the Wheels of
the breadth of Six Inches or upwards at the Bottom when drawn
by more than one Horse,Mule,Afs or other Beast the Sum of Three-pence **3**

AND when drawn by one Horse,Mule,Afs or other Beast the
Sum of Four-Pence (Except Carts) _____ **4**

FOR every Horse,Mule,Afs or other Beast drawing any Waggon
Wain,Cart or other such Carriage having the Fellies of the
Wheels of the Breadth of four inches and a half and lefs than
Six inches when drawn by more than one Horse,Mule,Afs or
other Beast the Sum of Three-pence three farthings _____ **$3\tfrac{3}{4}$**

AND when drawn by one Horse,Mule,Afs or other Beast the Sum
of Five-pence (Except Carts) _____ **5**

FOR every Horse,Mule,Afs or other Beast drawing any Cart with
Wheels of every Breadth when drawn by only one such Animal
the Sum of Six Pence _____ **6**

NB Two Oxen or neat Cattle drawing shall be considered as one Horse
3.G.4.C.126.

CARRIAGES with four Wheels arrixed to any Waggon or Cart
all as if drawn by two Horses,Carriages with two Wheels so
d pay Toll as if drawn by one Horse but such Carriages are
Tolls if conveying any Goods other than
for Protection.

Toll Board from Sussex
(from Harris - no date)

13

2.1 Toll Gates & Turnpikes

The turnpike trusts were generally empowered by their Acts of Parliament to 'erect or cause to be erected a gate or gates, turnpike or turnpikes', usually in positions that were left to their own discretion. Certain towns did lobby Parliament and as a result toll-gates could not be placed nearer than three miles distant so as not to discourage local markets. Trusts with linear routes therefore tended to have toll-gates at either end of their territory with occasional others inbetween, often where a side road joined the way. In contrast the town-centred trusts tended to end up with a ring of toll-gates around the outskirts guarding virtually every road inwards.

The trusts were however compelled to enforce a strictly defined set of toll charges that were to a large degree proportional to the amounts of damage caused by differing types of traffic. Local traffic was often favoured by being allowed a same day return trip at no extra cost and there were a number of common exemptions from toll, notably people going to church or to vote, agricultural traffic, the Army and mail coaches which sounded their horns on approaching the gates.

Most trusts had three main employees: a surveyor to initiate and oversee repairs together with a clerk and treasurer to administer their affairs. Their tasks were to engage labour as required to mend the roads and oversee the collectors employed at each toll-gate. There was an inherent weak link in the system here that depended on the honesty of the collectors or pike-men as they became known. This led in due course to the practice of toll-farming, whereby the proceeds of a toll-gate for the coming year were sold off by auction to 'toll-farmers', either individual collectors with initiative, or contractors who took on themselves the risk of employing several collectors. The trusts were thus assured of a toll income, which was often supplemented by composition payments from parishes who bought themselves out of their statutory labour obligations.

Toll Farming Poster, 1862
(from Serjeant & Penrose - 1973)

2.2 Toll-houses

To facilitate the twenty four hour presence of their collectors, the turnpike trusts usually built small associated dwellings at their gates:- the toll-houses. They generally comprised very minimal accommodation of two rooms with a scullery and privy attached, although larger types did become more common in later years. The larger ones were probably the result of toll farming, the houses being bid for at auction both as generators of toll income and as accommodation for the pike-men. These toll-houses were either one or two storeyed and thus came in many shapes and sizes, some trusts adopting a standard design whilst others seem to have tried many variations.

If built to a normal rectangular plan they would often have gable windows very close to the front corner of the building or a bay window on the main room to provide the collector with a view up and down the road. A development of the bay came in the form of the octagonal ended house where effectively the bay became the room, this particular form becoming the norm for the toll-house building-type to such an extent that it was also employed at toll collection points on the canals. The octagonal shape also appears in some country house park gatekeeper's lodges, where again an element of control was required.

It may thus have its roots in the neo-classical love of geometry or possibly may be derived from military precedents of a defensive nature, as many toll-houses of the more ornate 'gothick' kind sport the mock battlements of the picturesque. Wherever the shape derived from, it was nevertheless of great utility.

Much can be said for the presence of the buildings themselves; their many windows and forward position would undoubtedly have unsettled any approaching traveller intent on avoiding the toll with a feeling of having his every move watched. It is this presence that remains today as such a helpful clue to identifying toll-houses, particularly when they are not of the obvious octagonal type.

'Gothick' Gate-house, Rendlesham
photo: polystar

Whilst the pike-man's job required his presence on the premises it was not strictly necessary for him to be on guard looking out of the windows twenty four hours of the day. Most toll-houses were built on very small parcels of land owned by the trustees, usually carved out of the corners of fields, but sufficient to allow the tenants a small cottage garden for their home grown produce. Because of their usual remoteness these small plots often also contained their own well or pump for water supply.

Internally the toll-houses would have been very cramped by modern day standards, particularly if the pike-man had a family of any size. The small bedroom would have slept the whole family, a truckle bed for the children sliding out from beneath the main one, as can be seen at the Sussex toll-house at the Weald and Downland Museum. The other room served every other purpose, being in every sense the living room, and contained the hearth where food was cooked, together with seating, tables, storage etc. and may well have been awkward to furnish if without any square corners at all. The main door to the highway usually led off this room and it was often protected by a porch or shelter of some kind where the collector could receive tolls in the dry.

Another common indicative feature of toll-houses is a blank space where a toll-board would have been placed. This could be a filled in window at first floor or a space adjoining an asymmetrically placed door on the ground floor. Sited as they were hard against the highway, those that survive today are perhaps the most visible remains of the turnpike system. The keen industrial archaeologist will also be able to find many examples of milestones, a later requirement of the legislation, still shown as 'MS' on modern Ordnance Survey maps. There are also a few surviving gates, their general form consisting of a main vehicular gate or turnpike (originally a spiked pole), with usually a pedestrian gate between this and the toll-house.

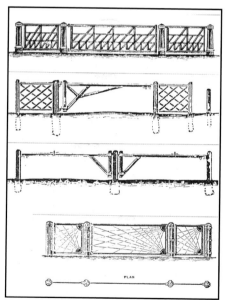

Varieties of Toll Gate
(from Searle - 1930)

2.3 Local Distinctiveness

A particular problem with toll-houses is dating their construction. In between a *terminus post quem* of the original turnpike act and a *terminus ante quem* of finding them on a tithe map or early Ordnance Survey lie many years. Most will be found to have been constructed nearer the earlier date at the beginning of a turnpike's existence and therefore not benefiting from the slightly improved communications that followed by overland transport. They were even less likely to have benefited from the greater improvements that the canals later brought to water borne transport, and certainly missed out on the radically changed face of building material distribution ushered in by the railway age.

In terms of their walling materials therefore, toll-houses were almost universally built of what was locally available and remain to this day useful pointers to local distinctiveness and the nature of the geology thereabouts. Thus in Plymouth we find the local Devonian limestone used, in Bath an Oolitic limestone, in Anglesey the local metamorphic rock and at Todmorden, in the Pennines, Millstone Grit. As eighteenth century buildings, where stone was not available, brick was usually the order of the day, so that in Cambridge we find white Gault bricks (see p.1), whilst in Essex red brick and tile from the London Clay.

Local Devonian Limestone Toll-house in Plymouth
(from Searle - 1930)

Although the timber-frame tradition had long gone into decline, and certainly was less suitable for forming an octagonal building, there is a timber-framed and thatched toll-house in Suffolk and the lap-boarded Sussex example in the Weald and Downland Museum, both of which are rectangular in plan.

Roofing materials show a similar pattern. Thatch was the material of an earlier age and unsuitable anyway as it required more frequent repair and maintenance, diverting the trust's funds away from the roads. It also represented a severe fire risk, especially in towns, a definite liability should there be any local dissent about the coming of the turnpikes. Pantiles and the larger stone flags and tiles were often the locally available preference. Whilst not best suited to the small areas of hipped roofs involved in octagonal buildings, they were sometimes used nevertheless, more so on the rectangular examples. Slate, however, was the new material of the age and seems to have been the predominant choice, even in the east where it had to be imported from afar. In the eighteenth century roofs were generally pitched according to the materials used, a slate or pantile roof requiring less timber at 30° to 40° pitch, than would a plaintile roof at 45° or more.

We have seen that toll-houses were basic small domestic buildings, housing persons fairly low down the social scale. As such they fit within the vernacular tradition, although the tendency has been for them to be studied as curiosities within the province of the industrial archaeologist. Within this vernacular tradition they may be considered somewhere near its later threshold, as particularly with the octagonal forms, there is an overlay of the 'polite', a signalling of their purpose as a particular type of building. This is especially true where a standard design marks their belonging to a particular trust or they venture into the 'picturesque' at the whim of the trustees. The fashionable input could manifest itself as 'gothick' windows or even crenellated parapets, which by this time presumably no longer required the King's licence.

These fashions were however directed from above, being very much the prerogative of the trustees, who as fashionable members of the gentry would have been very aware of the latest ideas and as keen to try them out on their turnpike roads as at their lodge gates. It is therefore possible that the octagonal form used in toll-houses derived from earlier garden buildings of this shape, as is believed to have happened with park lodge gatehouses. The turnpike roads can be seen in this light as a parallel phenomenon to the enclosures and creation of our country house estates. The gentry not only came to control large areas of land, signalling this benign stewardship with their various gatekeeper's lodges, but also the routes between the major centres, controlled by the toll-houses.

2.4 What Lies Ahead?

Local distinctiveness relates to the customs and ways of doing things that have evolved in an area, and which give it a distinctive local character. This 'difference from other places' appears not only in the landscape moulded by our management of the land but also in our built environment. An important part of maintaining local distinctiveness therefore involves celebrating the differences, keeping alive the stories and associations of a place.

The problem with toll-houses in this respect is their situation. They were mostly built in isolation, on the perimeters of our settlements and as a consequence almost never occur within our historic centres, where most modern day celebration of place happens. Whilst the turnpikes probably initiated ribbon development, encouraging the spread of suburban villas, their remains are now largely surrounded by it, so that apart from their intimate link with the actual road, toll-houses have little sense of place.

Unfortunately the road itself has become too fast and dangerous a place to encourage anyone to stop and wonder. Meanwhile our canals and railways, which move at a more human pace, have become the subjects of the majority of transport nostalgia, and thus leisure activity.

The major residual usage of toll-houses is as dwellings and as such they are cramped and therefore often extended; they are poorly serviced because of their remoteness and often unpleasantly sited on the highway edge. We therefore find our remaining toll-houses the unconsidered remnants of a forgotten system, infrequently listed unless tending towards the more 'polite' and severely at risk from future road developments.

In order to celebrate what is left, we need to take the first step in recognising it. Accordingly we will now look at Suffolk's turnpike roads and toll-houses in greater detail.

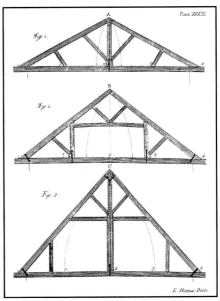

Varieties of Roof Pitch for Different Roofing Materials (from Cruickshank & Wyld - 1975)

19

3.0 The Suffolk Turnpikes

Stagecoach and Four
(from Smith - 1970)

Yoxford
13 July 1859

Sir,

    I am directed to inform you that the Trustees of the Turnpike assembled at a Meeting held here this day viewed the new Building now erecting by you in the Street and are of opinion that you have made an Encroachment upon the Road so as to reduce the original width thereof very nearly two feet. The Trustees feel that they cannot permit so great an Encroachment to pass by unnoticed and therefore have determined that unless you take down the Building and restore the Road to its original width within Ten days from this date they will cause the same to be taken down at your expense pursuant to the Powers vested in them by the General Turnpike Act.

          I am Sir
            Yours obediently
             B. B. Baas

Mr. A. B. Gray
  Brickmaker
  Yoxford.
                  Clerk to the Trustees

Turnpike Trust Letter, 1859
(from Serjeant & Penrose - 1973)

3.1 Suffolk Turnpike Trusts

Suffolk was fairly typical of the country as a whole in terms of turnpike activity through the eighteenth and early nineteenth centuries, its roads spread throughout the period with a just recognisable boom in the 1760's. Its first turnpike act was relatively early for the provinces and in 1711 connected the county town of Ipswich to Scole and Haughley, both outposts on the roads to Ipswich's nearest important neighbours, Norwich and Bury St. Edmunds respectively. Ipswich at that time was a prosperous market town with a large agricultural hinterland which had encouraged its growth as a port and in turn as a centre for shipbuilding.

Fifty years passed without further activity until in 1762 the act was passed for the Sudbury to Bury St. Edmunds turnpike. Further acts followed in the boom years, many making connections from close to the county borders at Newmarket or Haverhill to towns elsewhere. Those that were significantly within Suffolk included Thetford to Newmarket in 1768, with a branch off from Barton to Brandon in 1770, Scole to Bury St. Edmunds in 1769 and Bury St. Edmunds to Newmarket in 1770. Following the boom, activity continued at a fairly even pace. In 1785 the Ipswich to South Town linked to Great Yarmouth, via Lowestoft along what is now the A12 east coast road, and included a branch off to Bungay. The town-centred trust at Aldeburgh fed off this major route at three places in 1792, the same year that the Bury St. Edmunds to Cranwich road connected the former town northwards towards Thetford. In 1796 the Little Yarmouth to Blythburgh turnpike provided an alternative route in the north-east of the county via Beccles. 1802 saw Woodbridge connected to Eye and in 1812 the Ipswich to Helmingham linked into this route. In 1812 the Ipswich to Stratford St Mary road finally made the land link to Essex and London. Finally in 1828 Mildenhall was connected to Littleport near Ely. Although only one turnpike was actually town-centred, at the end of the day both Bury St. Edmunds and Ipswich had become hubs for many linear trusts.

Milestone, Woodbridge Road, Ipswich (*Ipswich - South Town*) photo: polystar

3.2 Chalk and Ice

Geologically Suffolk is for the most part underlain by chalk, the youngest and purest of limestones laid down in the Cretaceous period some 100 million years ago. It is however not the chalk of our high downlands, but rather of relatively low lying gently rolling countryside. The chalk and clay disappears in the far north-west beneath the recent peaty deposits of fenland. Within the chalk, and left as a deposit in its surface layer of clay, are found numerous flints, the silica rich nodules that have crystallised out separately from the original calcareous ooze that settled to form the chalk.

To the south, roughly along a line between Sudbury and Ipswich, the chalk dips beneath the later sands and clays of the London Clay, laid down during the Eocene period, about 50 million years ago. The river valleys of the Orwell and Deben, from Ipswich and Woodbridge respectively, have cut back through later crag deposits to expose these London Clay beds within which can be found septaria, large outcrops of a clayey limestone that was formerly used for both building and cement manufacture.

In the east of the county, however, both the Chalk and London Clay are buried beneath the more recent crag deposits, sands and clays of the Late Pliocene period, laid down in estuarine conditions preceding the Ice Ages of the last million years or so.

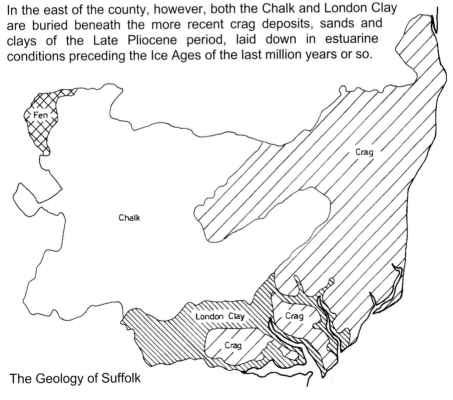

The Geology of Suffolk

3.3 Timber and Clay

In central and west Suffolk the chalk and crag deposits are covered by heavy glacial boulder clay soils, laid down during the Ice Ages of the Pleistocene period, so good for the wheat production that makes East Anglia the granary of Britain. There is thus a contrast between the heavy clay soils of 'High Suffolk' in the west and the lighter sandy soils of the eastern coastal strip, the 'Sandlings' that have become heathland through the leaching of nutrients that followed man's deforestation.

Whilst the sandlings were stripped of their cover fairly early on in man's history, the clay lands remained wooded to some extent right through to medieval times. This is largely due to the retention of woodland areas, managed on a cycle of coppicing to produce regular supplies of underwood and timber. However, by the sixteenth century with the period of timber frame construction at its peak, a shortage of timber meant that this Suffolk 'vernacular' only preserved a local tradition in building, much of its materials being imported from the Baltic. The underwood was still used for wattle and daub infill and the chalk of west Suffolk provided the raw material for a busy lime-burning industry. The local form that evolved was not one of exposed timber framing as seen in the west of England, but rather the more subtle use of lime renders and washes, the timber only appearing externally in jetties and exposed corner posts.

The presence of suitable clays meant that Suffolk figures relatively early in the rise of the popularity of brick. This was used occasionally to infill timber framing but really came into its own in the seventeenth and eighteenth centuries when many a timber-framed building was given a brick front, typically with a steep plaintiled roof tucked behind a parapet giving away the true construction. The bricks came in two main varieties, red or white, the former a very soft sandy brick, easily rubbed, the latter a harder buff coloured brick, both of which were often used together, one providing the detailed work to the other's use en masse.

Because Suffolk's chalk is geologically from the upper or middle strata, it was not very suitable for use as clunch, however its flint, pebbles and cobbles were often used as a facing material usually combined with red brick quoins and dressings. These materials come lower down the social scale as does the use of the heavy boulder clay in the north-west of Suffolk for clay lump construction, a form of prefabricated cob.

3.4 Suffolk Toll-houses

Suffolk's first toll-houses along the Ipswich to Scole, Haughley etc. turnpike of 1711 were early, even by national standards. That at Claydon is a simple rectangular two storey house of brick, now rendered, with a clay pantile roof. Although not octagonal and looking like an adaptation of an existing building, it was purpose-built, as revealed by its proximity to the highway and the presence of small gable windows giving views up and down the road. At nearby Great Blakenham, on the Bury branch of the same turnpike, the now demolished toll-house was set gable end onto the road with a central doorway.

The Sudbury to Bury St. Edmunds turnpike of 1762 provides Suffolk's best known toll-house at Sicklesmere. It is of the expected octagonal shape in the local white brick with rubbed white brick pointed window heads and a slate roof wrapped around an octagonal chimney. A similar single storey example, again octagonal in white brick and slate, is to be found at Botesdale on the Scole to Bury St. Edmunds road of 1769, although this one was also reputedly a park lodge and would appear more likely to date from the 1820's with its double arched round headed windows. Both these are atypical of the county as a whole.

Single storey rectangular brick construction seems to have been the norm especially in the east, as adopted by the Ipswich to South Town turnpike of 1785, with their typical bungalow shapes and gabled pantile roofs. This type accords with both the rectangular tradition of timber frame construction and allowed the use of the locally available pantiles without the need for difficult hip details. The example at Carlton was the model adopted by the Yoxford to Aldeburgh turnpike trustees in 1792 for their toll-houses, each costing £93 and put up by a bricklayer and a carpenter. The Little Yarmouth to Blythburgh turnpike of 1796 seems also to have adopted a similar pattern as can be seen in the toll-house at Haddiscoe.

Toll-house Window, Claydon
(*Ipswich - Scole, Haughley etc*)
photo: polystar

1793 saw the completion of Suffolk's only sizeable man-made waterway, the Ipswich to Stowmarket Navigation, which was essentially the canalisation of the existing river Gipping. This probably helped with the bulk distribution of grain from Suffolk's agricultural hinterland through the docks at Ipswich, but probably had little effect on turnpike traffic.

Turnpike activity continued and later, in 1802, the Woodbridge to Eye turnpike saw a return to the Claydon model for its toll-houses, with rectangular two storey cottages of render and pantiles, that at Eye revealing its former purpose where the render over an original central doorway is cracked, the crack even outlining a steeply pitched porch over. These foursquare buildings are very much the norm in central and western Suffolk.

In 1812 the Ipswich to Helmingham turnpike adopted a mixture of one and two storey toll-houses, of no standard design but all of brick with slate or tile roofs. The continuing importance of Ipswich as a port is shown by the fact that it was not until this same date that the Ipswich to Stratford St. Mary turnpike finally made a toll road connection out of the county towards London. The red brick toll-house at its far end was actually just over the bridge at Dedham in Essex and constructed with a plaintiled gambrel roof containing the first floor, not unusual in itself, but perhaps so hipped around an octagonal end.

Perhaps the most striking thing that emerges about Suffolk's toll-houses is that they do not seem to follow any particular pattern, no two that remain are the same, even within the same turnpike trust. In addition there is a decided scarcity of what might be considered the 'normal' octagonal form more prevalent in the west.

As a result of this, after the following gazetteer section describing the county's toll-houses, there will be found an appendix illustrating other octagonal buildings around the county - they do exist, it is just that they are not toll-houses.

Side Window Detail, Mildenhall Fen
(*Mildenhall - Littleport etc.*)
photo: polystar

4.0 A Suffolk Gazetteer

The remainder of this book comprises a gazetteer of both toll-houses and their former sites. In general all surviving toll-houses are illustrated and given a map reference without brackets. Those that have been lost, but where a suitable photograph has been forthcoming, are also illustrated but given bracketed references. The remaining toll-house sites, lost completely without trace other than documentary, are described as far as possible in the boxes at the foot of each page. Those that appeared as 'T.G.' on the first edition Ordnance Survey maps of c.1838 are so marked.

The gazetteer starts in the far north-west of the county, runs across Suffolk to the south-east and then concludes by filling in the north-east corner with its links across part of Norfolk to Great Yarmouth. Purists may question the validity of including a few from just into Cambridgeshire or over the Stour or Waveney, but they are there for completeness; no county stands alone.

The author is very conscious of this being a first attempt to document these buildings in such detail and would be very grateful to hear of any errors, omissions, additional information or photographic evidence in respect of any toll-house that readers might be aware of.

Readers should be aware that most of our surviving toll-houses are now in private ownership as people's homes, please respect this. The author apologises in advance to any owners for any nuisance this publication might bring their way, and hopes the benefits of wider knowledge of this obscure subject can be seen to outweigh any inconvenience caused.

It is certainly hoped that a good many owners will come to appreciate their guardianship of this small part of our heritage, and perhaps a few more of these unique buildings will in due course get the added protection of becoming listed buildings, rather than become subjects of memorials like the adjoining illustration.

Memorial Stone for Burwell Ness
Toll-house, Cambridgeshire
photo: polystar

27

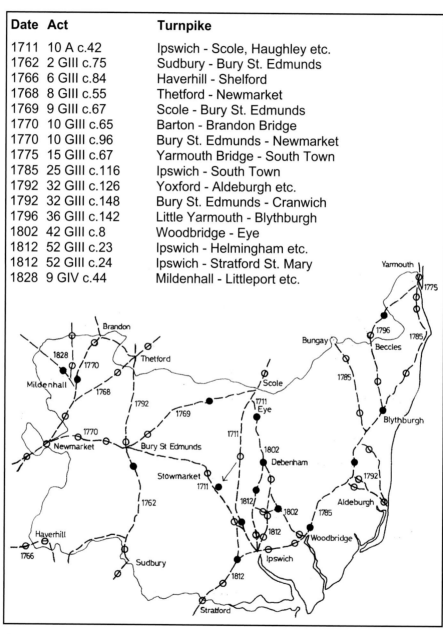

Date	Act	Turnpike
1711	10 A c.42	Ipswich - Scole, Haughley etc.
1762	2 GIII c.75	Sudbury - Bury St. Edmunds
1766	6 GIII c.84	Haverhill - Shelford
1768	8 GIII c.55	Thetford - Newmarket
1769	9 GIII c.67	Scole - Bury St. Edmunds
1770	10 GIII c.65	Barton - Brandon Bridge
1770	10 GIII c.96	Bury St. Edmunds - Newmarket
1775	15 GIII c.67	Yarmouth Bridge - South Town
1785	25 GIII c.116	Ipswich - South Town
1792	32 GIII c.126	Yoxford - Aldeburgh etc.
1792	32 GIII c.148	Bury St. Edmunds - Cranwich
1796	36 GIII c.142	Little Yarmouth - Blythburgh
1802	42 GIII c.8	Woodbridge - Eye
1812	52 GIII c.23	Ipswich - Helmingham etc.
1812	52 GIII c.24	Ipswich - Stratford St. Mary
1828	9 GIV c.44	Mildenhall - Littleport etc.

The Turnpike Roads of Suffolk

Mildenhall Fen Toll-house
TL 679779   'T.G.'
Mildenhall - Littleport etc.

photo: polystar

This small bungalow type toll-house at Stock Corner on the A1101, to the north-west of what is now Mildenhall Airfield, is in fact fairly typical of Suffolk toll-houses, as we shall see in the following pages.

It gives away its purpose with its small windows set near the corner of the gables, each only a few inches square, which allow views from within along the road in both directions. Constructed of flint with brick dressings, its original roof has now been replaced with concrete tiles.

As indicated above it appeared on the first edition 1" Ordnance Survey maps as 'T.G.'

Eriswell Toll-house
(TL 712783)   'T.G.'
Mildenhall - Littleport etc.

Just north of Mildenhall on what is now a minor road, there was once a toll-house near Eriswell. It was just around a corner past where a track called Slack's Drove heads off northwards.

It controlled the beginning of a route northwards from here through Lakenheath towards Hockwold, just inside Norfolk, and was shown on the 1882 first edition 25" Ordnance Survey map as 'T.P.'

Paper Mills Toll-house (Cambs)
TL 473595   'T.G.'
Godmanchester - Newmarket Heath

photo: polystar

The Godmanchester to Newmarket turnpike formed the western fork of the road south-west out of Newmarket towards Cambridge, later becoming the A1303.

At its end on the approach to Cambridge, understandably in Newmarket Road, stands the Paper Mills toll-house, built of local Cambridge white bricks with a slate roof.

It is single storey with a large octagonal ended bay containing a doorway facing the road, and is now known as The Round House.

Newmarket Heath Toll-house
(TL 619614)   'T.G.'
Newmarket Heath - Chesterford

About two miles out of Newmarket, roughly on the border with Cambridgeshire where the road crosses 'Devil's Ditch', there once stood a toll-house controlling the south-western approaches to the town.

Here the road forked, the south-western leg forming the Newmarket to Chesterford turnpike, which later became the A1304/A11 leading ultimately to London.

30

Littleport Bridge Toll-house (Cambs)
TL 578877   'T.P.'
Mildenhall - Littleport etc.

photo: polystar

The turnpike road north-westwards from Mildenhall continues for many miles almost dead straight once past Stock Corner. It soon crosses the county border and continues in its flat Fenland manner until it crosses the river Great Ouse at Littleport Bridge.

Here on the east bank, there stands the other toll-house that controlled this particular trust's road, now luckily by-passed because the road bridge has been moved downstream slightly.

It is brick built with a recessed panel for the toll-board (now painted to look like a window) and at least one useful small side window.

Wilton Bridge Toll-house
(TL 724868)   'T.G.'
Mildenhall - Littleport etc.

The northern end of the road from Lakenheath to Hockwold was controlled by a toll-house just over the Norfolk border adjoining Wilton Bridge.

This now appears to have been lost and may have gone when the bridge was rebuilt: the current bridge is not the 'Suspension Bridge' shown on the first edition 1" O.S. maps, just south of the designation 'T.G.'

Four Lost Breckland Toll-houses

Thetford - Newmarket

Bury St Edmunds

Freckenham Toll-house
(TL 693698)   'T.G.'
Thetford - Newmarket

The Thetford to Newmarket turnpike road was also controlled by toll-houses at either end. About four miles north-east of Newmarket there was a toll-house at Red Lodge, just inside the Suffolk border, and just inside the parish of Freckenham.

It stood on the north-west side of the road on a section of the A11 that has now been by-passed, so that its loss may have been premature.

Snailwell Toll-house
(TL 655648)   'T.G.'
Bury St Edmunds - Newmarket

The former toll-house at Snailwell, about a mile north-east of Newmarket, was another one built right on the county boundary with Cambridgeshire.

Also known as Moulton Gate, it was on the north-western side of the road just where it forked into the Bury St Edmunds and Thetford branches. Thus controlling the north-eastern approach to the town, it may well have served the Thetford to Newmarket turnpike as well.

Elveden Toll-house
(TL 820798)   'T.G.'
Thetford - Newmarket

The northern end of this road was similarly controlled by a toll-house about four miles south-west of Thetford, this time at Elveden. It too stood on the north-west side of the road, very near where a lodge now stands on the south-east side (see appendix p.58).

It appeared on the 1841 tithe map, described in the apportionment as 'Toll Gate House', but listed as in the ownership of the Glebe.

Bury St Edmunds Toll-house
(TL 851660)
Bury St Edmunds - Cranwich

Set back from the site of the toll-house that once controlled the road northwards out of Bury St Edmunds, 'The Tollgate' public house is but one of several local remembrances of the former use. Nearby can be found 'Tollgate Bridge', mentioned on the first edition 25" Ordnance Survey map, and not far away there is still Tollgate Lane.

The tithe map of 1840 also shows 'The Toll Gate', but today nothing remains of this toll-house.

Mildenhall Woods Toll-house
TL 729758   'T.G.'
Barton - Brandon Bridge

photo: polystar

To the north-east of Mildenhall, there survives another toll-house, this one guarding the A1065 road to Brandon. Now adjoining Mildenhall Woods, it was marked on earlier maps as 'Tollgate Cottage' , the woods then known as 'Tollgate Plantation'.

It sits where a side road from Mildenhall itself joins the turnpike road running north from Barton Mills. It is of two storey brick construction, now painted, with dormers and a porch facing the road. On the north gable return there are signs of a small opening having been bricked up.

Brandon Toll-house
(TL 766850)   'T.G.'
Barton - Brandon Bridge

Although there is a likely looking estate lodge known as 'London Lodge' slightly nearer the town (see appendix p. 57), nothing remains today of the former toll-house that once guarded the south-western approach towards Brandon from Mildenhall.

Like many other lost toll-houses this one was presumably demolished to make way for road improvements.

Higham 'Toll-house Cottage'
TL 746661
(Bury St Edmunds - Newmarket)

photo: polystar

Although listed grade II and described in its listing as a former toll-house, this roadside cottage with a blocked doorway facing the road at Higham is probably an impostor and perhaps rightly belongs in the appendix to this book.

With its truncated pentagonal plan and 'gothick' windows it certainly looks the part, and is definitely of the right period. The problem is that none of the early maps or turnpike records indicate a toll-house here. The Gazeley parish tithe map of 1840 shows it as 'Round Lodge', its occupiers and owners being private citizens rather than the usual turnpike trust.

Kentford Toll-house
(TL 709668)   'T.G.'
Bury St Edmunds - Newmarket

The village of Kentford, four miles east of Newmarket was the site of another toll-house, situated on the north-east side of the B1506 at a crossroads. It was presumably demolished to make way for the modern houses that now fill the site: nos. 1, 2 and 3 Tollgate Place.

Shown on the 1842 tithe map as 'Toll Gate', it is listed in the apportionment for the village as 'Toll House', owned by 'Trustees of Bury and Newmarket Turnpike Road'.

Botesdale Toll-house
TM 053763
Scole - Bury St Edmunds

photo: polystar

With its round-headed windows, white brick, probably from Woolpit, and slate roof this toll-house has 1820 or thereabouts written all over it. The toll-house is grade II listed, the description giving it as a former lodge and toll-house c.1770.

It also appears on the 1839 tithe apportionment as simply 'House & Garden', although its ownership is listed there as 'Trustees of the Turnpike'.

This is probably second only to Sicklesmere (qv) amongst the octagonal toll-houses in Suffolk, although as we are seeing, these are far from typical in this county.

Risby Toll-house
(TL 820654)   'T.G.'
Bury St Edmunds - Newmarket

Somewhere just to the west of Bury St Edmunds, underneath the dual carriageway of the current A14, lies the site of the former Risby toll-house. It was just inside that parish on the boundary with Westley.

It was shown as 'Risby Toll Gate' on the tithe map of c.1840. The apportionment gives it as 'Toll Gate House & Premises' owned by 'Trustees of Bury & Newmarket Turnpike'.

'Tollgate' at Ixworth
TL 931699
(Scole - Bury St Edmunds)

photo: polystar

On the southern approaches to Ixworth, actually in the parish of Pakenham, there is this small bungalow called 'Tollgate'. It certainly is fairly typical of Suffolk's toll-houses, very near the road and on a bend with good views up and down the road.

The problem is that the old turnpike records do not mention a toll-gate here, and the tithe map has it as a privately owned 'Cottage & Garden'.

This may well be a toll-house, perhaps used only for a short period, so it is included here rather than in the appendix.

Great Barton Toll-house
(TL 902675)   'T.G.'
Scole - Bury St Edmunds

Apart from Botesdale, the other main toll-gate on the Scole to Bury St Edmunds turnpike was at Great Barton, now demolished. It stood at a cross-roads east of the village opposite the Bunbury Arms public house.

About three miles nearer Bury St Edmunds to the west, the first edition 1" Ordnance Survey map also shows 'T.P.' at a point now covered by a roundabout (TL 872652).

Sicklesmere Toll-house
TL 877608   'T.G.'
Sudbury - Bury St Edmunds

photo: polystar

Even in a national context, the toll-house at Sicklesmere, just south of Bury St Edmunds on the A134 Sudbury road, is one of our best remaining examples of octagonal toll-house and is thus listed grade II.

It is however strangely atypical in Suffolk. Built of white brick (probably from Woolpit or Sudbury) with 'gothick' arched windows and a slate roof, the octagonal shape advertises its purpose well. The photograph shows it prior to the recent window replacement and porch removal.

It appeared on the tithe map as 'Turnpike Gate', described in the apportionment as 'Toll Gate House' owned by 'Trustees of Turnpike'.

Rodbridge Toll-house
(TL 859439)   'T.G.'
Sudbury - Bury St Edmunds

The road southwards towards Sudbury had one further gate at Rodbridge. It was situated at the crossroads now known as Rodbridge Corner, just south of Long Melford, the adjoining plot having been listed as 'Tollgate Pightle' in the tithe apportionment.

The first edition 1" Ordnance Survey map also shows a further toll-house site marked 'T.G.' near Sudbury, situated at Bulmer Tye, about a mile into Essex on the south-west side (TL 849389).

Dedham Toll-house (Essex)
(TM 043334)   'T.G.'
Ipswich - Stratford St Mary

Just over the border into Essex, across the River Stour, there once stood a toll-house, controlling the road from Ipswich onwards towards London. As such it is probably better attributed to an Essex turnpike trust. The name of the nearby Talbooth Inn commemorates its former existence.

Constructed of local red brick and tile, it has the octagonal shape, but this is lost somewhat with the large mansard roof dominating its shape.

Its position relative to the road is shown to good effect on this old post-card sent in 1936.

Withersfield Toll-house
(TL 653477)   'T.G.'
Haverhill - Shelford

Records indicate that a toll-house once stood in the centre of the village of Withersfield, controlling the start of the Red Cross turnpike from Haverhill into Cambridgeshire. The tithe map apportionment of 1840 listed it as 'Turnpike House & Garden', owned by 'Trustees of Turnpike Road'.

A further toll-house on this road stood further along at Horseheath (TL 633469), also appearing as 'T.G.' on the first edition 1" Ordnance Survey map.

Copdock Toll-house
TM 119422
Ipswich - Stratford St Mary

photo: polystar

Formerly known as Copdock Gate, this toll-house adjoins the boundary with the parish of Washbrook, on the south-western approaches to Ipswich. It is probably constructed of brick, now rendered, and has a hipped slate roof.

A long thin bungalow, it has a gable window at each end looking up and down the road, confirming the building's previous use. It seems likely that the central of the current three windows facing the road was at one time the doorway.

Although not described on the earlier Ordnance Survey maps, recent editions show it as 'Tollgate Lodge'.

Lattinford Toll-house
(TM 082371)   'T.G.'
Ipswich - Stratford St Mary

Unusual in what we have seen so far, this particular turnpike road had a mid-way gate, a feature we will find more common on the longer routes. It was situated at Lattinford Hill and has now been demolished, presumably for widening of the A12 into dual carriageway.

It is mentioned in Turnpike Trust returns in the early 1820's.

Great Blakenham Toll-house
(TM 118508)   'T.G.'
Ipswich - Scole, Haughley etc.

This old photograph from Suffolk Record Office shows the former toll-house at Great Blakenham. It stood at the foot of Chalk Hill Lane on the west side of what is now the B1113 (formerly the A45).

It was a single storey bungalow type, but unusually here turned at 90° to the road. The sign of the adjacent Chequers public house is clearly visible, as is Tollgate Farm in the background. There are no signs of any gates in the picture, but there appears to be a toll-board still on the wall of the building by the window.

The tithe map apportionment of 1840 described it as 'Toll House' owned by 'Trustees of Turnpike'.

Stowmarket Toll-house
(TM 038603)   'T.G.'
Ipswich - Scole, Haughley etc.

Further north up this western branch of the Ipswich - Scole, Haughley etc. turnpike, there was a further toll-house just north of the town of Stowmarket. It was on the west side of the road near Spikes Lane, and was probably demolished for road widening when the A45 (now A14) was made dual carriageway.

It is shown as 'Old Tollgate' on an old 6" Ordnance Survey map and appeared on the tithe map of 1839, described as 'Toll House' owned by 'Turnpike Trustees'.

Claydon Toll-house
TM 130502   'T.G.'
Ipswich - Scole, Haughley etc.

photo: polystar

The northern branch of this turnpike trust's roads had a toll-house, just past where the western branch left for Great Blakenham, in the village of Claydon.

This substantial two storey building on the parish boundary with Barham sits close to the highway edge and gives away its purpose with the small side windows in the gables for visibility up and down the road. Constructed of brick, now rendered, with a clay pantile roof, it is similar to several toll-houses we shall see in the following pages.

The 1838 tithe apportionment lists it as 'Toll House' owned by 'Trustees of Turnpike'.

Thelveton Toll-house (Norfolk)
(TM 161808)   'T.G.'
Norwich - Scole Bridge

Another Tollgate Farm can be found on modern maps just north of Scole, where the A140 Ipswich to Scole road continues northwards towards Norwich.

The site has now been by-passed by the Dickleburgh relief road and the toll-house presumably belonged to the above-mentioned Norfolk trust.

Brockford Toll-house
(TM 119648)　　'T.G.'
Ipswich - Scole, Haughley etc.

photo: stowe veterinary group

Yet another Tollgate Farm can still be found on the A140 near the village of Brockford. Near here the 'Toll-gate House' described in the tithe apportionment of 1841 once stood close to the highway edge. This toll-house itself replaced an earlier one three miles to the south at Stonham Parva.

A unique survival, this timber-framed, plastered and thatched toll-house was bodily transported seven miles south to a new site near Needham Market in 1972.

Much extended, it now forms part of a veterinary surgery, known locally as the Mustard Pot (see p.67).

Witnesham Toll-house
(TM 182538)　　'T.G.'
Ipswich - Helmingham etc.

Once the earlier Ipswich to Scole road had been joined by the Woodbridge to Eye road in 1802, it soon became necessary to control the northern hinterland of Ipswich between the two routes.

Hence the Ipswich to Helmingham Turnpike Trust of 1812, with one of its main toll-houses at the Ashbocking B1077/B1078 cross-roads, in the parish of Witnesham. This appeared as 'Tollhouse' on the tithe apportionment of 1844, owned by 'Trustees of Turnpike'.

Whitton Toll-house
(TM 161483)   'T.G.'
Ipswich - Helmingham etc.

photo: polystar

The toll-house at Whitton, sitting well forward on a minor road north of Ipswich heading for Henley, was unfortunately lost to a fire in 2001, and has now been replaced by a modern house set further back on the plot.

This photograph shows it in the early 1990's, having already lost its doorway which was presumably on the gabled elevation facing the main road. The lane adjoining heads eastwards off this north-south route to Westerfield.

The tithe apportionment of 1840 lists it as 'Toll House', owned by 'Turnpike, Trustees of the'.

Westerfield Toll-house
(TM 174477)   'T.G.'
Ipswich - Helmingham etc.

At the end of the lane from Whitton Toll-house, at the cross-roads in Westerfield there was once a further toll-house. This was on another north-south road from Ipswich, now the B1077, this time towards Witnesham.

Now long gone, it too had appeared on the tithe map, the apportionment of 1839 listing it as 'Tollhouse', owned by 'Turnpike Trustees'.

Crowfield Toll-house
TM 157581   'T.G.'
Ipswich - Helmingham etc.

photo: polystar

Continuing northwards from the Whitton toll-house, through the village of Henley, the road eventually goes through Crowfield before joining the Woodbridge to Eye road just south of Debenham.

Here there remains a toll-house, shown on the tithe apportionment of 1838 as 'Toll Gate House', owned by 'Trustees of Roads'.

The building is of two storeys and rendered, probably on brick, with a slate roof. It appears to have on its southern side, around what is now a window, a stone slab porch construction, not unlike those found in Cornwall.

Henley Toll-house
(TM 173534)
Ipswich - Helmingham etc.

On the B1078, about half a mile west of the Witnesham toll-house at Ashbocking cross-roads, early 6" Ordnance Survey maps showed another 'Tollgate House' at what is known as Hare and Hounds Corner.

It was only shown as 'Cottage' on the tithe map apportionment of 1838 and is actually in the parish of Henley, although like the Witnesham example, it would appear to be in Ashbocking.

Otley Bottom Toll-house
TM 205542
Ipswich - Helmingham etc.

photo: polystar

The toll-house at Otley Bottom controlled the point at which the B1078 road eastwards from Ashbocking cross-roads met the Woodbridge to Eye turnpike, now the B1079.

Now known as Elm Cottage, it can only be described as having one and a half storeys, with two dormer windows, each over a ground floor window facing the road. Presumably at one time it had a doorway on this elevation.

There was also reputedly a further toll-house in Otley, controlling a side lane about a mile further north at TM 202555.

Bredfield Toll-house
(TM 261499)
Woodbridge - Eye

North-west of Woodbridge, the 1841 tithe map showed 'Toll House Cottage' at the end of Hasketon Road. This controlled the beginning of the Woodbridge to Eye turnpike.

Situated on a T-junction, now cut off from the town, the wrong side of the by-pass, the site is covered with fairly mature trees and all that can be determined is the diagonal line of the rear boundary of the small corner plot, now a low earthen bank.

Debenham Toll-house
TM 176643
Woodbridge - Eye

photo: polystar

This render and pantile house, known as 'Tollgate Cottage', on the B1077 Aspall road just north of Debenham, might seem debatable as a toll-house.

Turnpike records indicate a toll-house at Debenham, but the one so-called in the village is probably a market toll house, rather than a turnpike one (see appendix pp.63 and 71).

This building however, is fairly near the edge of the highway and compares favourably with the toll-house at Eye shown opposite, especially if one imagines the central window as a doorway.

Framsden Toll-house
(TM 194595)
Woodbridge - Eye

Another slightly doubtful site is that at Framsden, on the B1077 south of Debenham.

Here early 6" Ordnance Survey maps show 'Tollgate Corner', whilst the tithe apportionment, as with the Debenham example adjoining, lists only a 'Cottage'.

The site was however mentioned in Turnpike Trust returns in the early 1820's, and may have been just a gate without a toll-house.

Eye Toll-house
TM 148736
Woodbridge - Eye

photo: polystar

Immediately to the south of the town of Eye, at the northern end of this particular route is another 'Tollgate Cottage'.

This was shown on the early 6" Ordnance Survey map as 'Old Toll House' and was also mentioned in Turnpike Trust returns. It was also just listed as 'Cottage' on the tithe map apportionment of 1839.

It confirms its former use with its small side windows near the front of the gables and the outline of a former porch to a toll-collector's doorway, now blocked in, but faintly discernible up close as fine cracks in the render.

Rushmere Toll-house
(TM 204454)
Ipswich - South Town

The first toll-house out of Ipswich to the east, was at Rushmere, at the junction of the main A12 and Bent Lane just north of Rushmere Heath. Now the site of a modern bungalow, it was shown on the tithe apportionment as 'Toll Gate, House' occupied by 'Trustees of Turnpike Road', and on the early 25" O.S. map as 'Old Tollgate'.

Two further gates were also shown as 'T.G.' on early 1" maps nearer Ipswich: one at Rushmere Road roundabout (TM 182452), the other further east at Heath Road roundabout (TM 194452).

Melton Toll-house
TM 284510   'T.G.'
Ipswich - South Town

photo: polystar

The eastern side of Woodbridge also had a toll-house on the old A12, just outside the village of Melton

This one still remains, although at present the roof is being rebuilt and the front wing had been partially rebuilt following a car collision some years ago. The windows and doors have been replaced, but in their original openings, and the brickwork has been painted.

It appeared on the tithe map, the apportionment listing 'Tollhouse' owned by 'Trustees of Turnpike Road'.

Martlesham Toll-house
(TM 253475)
Ipswich - South Town

On the western approaches to Woodbridge there was at one time a toll-house at Martlesham near the bridge over the creek and the junction with Sandy Lane.

Now long gone, it was shown on the tithe apportionment of 1838 as 'Toll Gate Cottage'. Had it remained it would now be sited in a relatively quiet backwater as the main road now by-passes Martlesham village.

Carlton Toll-house
TM 386637   'T.G.'
Ipswich - South Town

photo: polystar

Another 'Suffolk bungalow' type toll-house, this one at Carlton just north of Saxmundham, is sadly the victim of creeping modernisation.

Since this photograph was taken in the early 1990's it has lost its windows to double glazing, had its doorway blocked up, its toll collector's canopy removed, and is now slowly being clad in stained lap boarding. Such sensitive restoration could so easily be the fate of numerous other unlisted toll-houses illustrated herein, and should be a warning to us all.

It appeared on the 1840 tithe map apportionment as 'Tollgate House' owned by 'Trustees of Turnpike'.

Benacre Toll-house
(TM 504851)   'T.G.'
Ipswich - South Town

Further north still on this longest of Suffolk turnpikes there was a toll-house at Benacre, just south of Lowestoft. It stood on a site now by-passed by road improvements.

It was listed in Turnpike Trust returns of the early 1820's and featured on the tithe map apportionment of 1840 as 'Toll House' owned by 'Trustees of Turnpike Road'. It was also shown on the first edition 25" Ordnance Survey map of 1884 (sheet 19/10) as 'Old Toll House'.

Four More Lost Toll-houses

Ipswich - South Town

Wenhaston Toll-house
(TM 391762)   'T.G.'
Ipswich - South Town

The A144 road northwards off the A12 from near Darsham, towards Bungay on the Norfolk border, was formerly a branch of the Ipswich to South Town turnpike.

At its southern end this branch was controlled by a toll-house at Wenhaston just south of the town of Halesworth. It appeared on the 1839 tithe apportionment as owned by 'Turnpike, Trustees for the', but was only described as 'Cottage'.

Hopton Toll-house
(TG 525001)   'T.G.'
Ipswich - South Town

The final northern stretch of the Ipswich to South Town road had two toll-houses between Lowestoft and Great Yarmouth, both now lost.

The southern one was about midway between the two towns at Hopton on a site now by-passed by the modern road.

It appeared on the first edition 25" Ordnance Survey map (sheet 4/3) as 'Old Toll House'.

St Johns Toll-house
(TM 360876)   'T.G.'
Ipswich - South Town

The northern end of this branch road also had a toll-house, that at St Johns Ilketshall, on the A144 just south of Bungay.

It too appeared on the tithe map, but as 'Toll House', and was mentioned in Turnpike Trust returns in the early 1820's.

Gorleston Toll-house
(TG 520018)   'T.G.'
Ipswich - South Town

About a mile north of the Hopton toll-house, there was another on the southern outskirts of Gorleston, also now demolished. Both of these northern toll-houses were originally in Suffolk, but now are part of Norfolk.

It too appeared on the first edition 25" Ordnance Survey map of 1885 (sheet 2/15) as 'Old Toll House'.

Blythburgh Toll-house
TM 453754   'T.G.'
Ipswich - South Town

photo: polystar

Between Carlton and Benacre, there was a further toll-house at Blythburgh, from where another turnpike trust route headed off northwards to Great Yarmouth via Beccles (qv).

Like many toll-houses in this area it was shown on the tithe apportionment as simply 'Cottage', although owned by 'Turnpike, Trustees for the'. It was also mentioned in Turnpike Trust returns of the early 1820's.

This difficult to photograph brick bungalow, behind a fence close to the highway edge, is known as 'Tollgate Cottage'. Some windows and doorways are blocked up, so that it now faces the lane at the rear.

South Town Toll-house
(TG 521075)
South Town

A separate turnpike trust appears to have been created for the final mile or so of road northwards from South Town across the river to Great Yarmouth. This had its own toll-house at South Town on the south-western bank of the river, but nothing remains of it.

There are a number of other toll-house sites around the northern approaches to Great Yarmouth where the 'Acle Straight' came in from Norwich.

'Tollgate' on site of Snape Toll-house
(TM 385598)
Yoxford - Aldeburgh etc.

photo: polystar

This small bungalow called 'Tollgate' on the A1094 just west of Snape is not a toll-house, and should perhaps appear in the appendix. It is however built within a plot, on the corner of which a toll-house did at one time stand.

The toll-house itself appeared as 'Tollgate' on the tithe map of 1848, but was listed simply as 'Cottage'. It controlled one of the three routes off the main A12 converging on the seaside town of Aldeburgh, known collectively as the Aldeburgh Turnpike.

It also appeared on the first O.S. maps, nothing being shown in 1904 or 1927 and later editions showing the new bungalow.

> ### Sternfield Toll-house
> (TM 39?48?)
> *Yoxford - Aldeburgh etc.*
>
> The second approach to Aldeburgh from the west was mid-way between the Snape and Middleton roads, passing through the village of Sternfield near Saxmundham.
>
> Here there was also a toll-house, but its exact siting is still a little uncertain, and no trace seems to remain today.

Middleton Toll-house
(TM 414678)   'T.G.'
Yoxford - Aldeburgh etc.

photo: janet barnes

This photograph from c.1960 shows the rear of the former toll-house at Middleton Moor, apparently similar in design to that at Carlton. It was rebuilt there in about 1824, having originally been sited, twenty years earlier, a few hundred yards further east along the Yoxford road.

Demolished c.1970, a small bungalow now occupies the plot, known as 'Tollgate Cottage'.

The toll-house appeared on the 1839 tithe apportionment as simply 'Cottage', but is shown as owned by 'Aldeburgh Turnpike'. Turnpike Trust minutes of October 1806 speak of the 'newly created gate at Middleton'.

Brampton Toll-house
(TM 435822)
Little Yarmouth - Blythburgh

The A145 road off the A12 northwards from Blythburgh to Beccles and beyond was originally part of the Little Yarmouth turnpike, providing an alternative inland route to Great Yarmouth.

The first toll-house here was at Brampton, shown as 'House', owned by 'Yarmouth Turnpike Trustees' on the tithe map apportionment of 1838. Turnpike Trust minutes of April 1796 record 'order placed for construction of turnpike and toll house for the sum of £98, at Beccles side of cross-roads to Stoven'.

'Toll House' on site of Aldeburgh Toll-house
(TM 458570)
Yoxford - Aldeburgh etc.

photo: polystar

The western approaches to Aldeburgh were controlled by a toll-house near where the Middleton road branches off from the Snape road to the west of the town.

Now demolished this was shown on the tithe apportionment as 'Tollgate House', but owned by 'Aldborough Corporation', rather than the usual trustees. Turnpike Trust minutes of June 1792 speak of a toll-house 'upon the same scale, dimensions and scantlings as Carlton Toll House...for the sum of £93, to be complete by 3rd August', i.e. a single storey building.

The building there now, used as a B&B, is of two storeys and probably dates from the early 20th Century.

Southwold Toll-house?
TM 507758
(Ipswich - South Town)

A possibly private toll-house may have controlled the road out of Southwold harbour, where it forks at the foot of South Green, before ascending to the town, eventually joining the main east coast road from Ipswich to South Town.

Today the most likely looking building there is called Coachman's Cottage, 18th Century of two bays tight against the road with a central doorway. Interestingly it does have a suitable small side window facing the harbour, although more recent houses now obscure the view.

Haddiscoe Toll-house (Norfolk)
TM 446970   'T.G.'
Little Yarmouth - Blythburgh

photo: polystar

Here we have the final toll-house on the Little Yarmouth Turnpike at Haddiscoe, relatively well preserved with its giveaway side windows and a large new window where the near central collector's doorway had been.

Very similar to the Carlton example, in the Suffolk 'bungalow' tradition, this is probably what the Brampton and Gillingham examples were like.

It too appeared in Turnpike Trust minutes of April 1796: 'order placed for construction of turnpike and toll house, for sum of £98, at south end of Haddiscoe Dam', which is precisely where we find it today.

Gillingham Toll-house (Norfolk)
(TM 412917)   'T.G.'
Little Yarmouth - Blythburgh

North of Brampton the Little Yarmouth route crossed over the Waveney into Norfolk, once past Beccles. Here there was a toll-house described in Turnpike Trust minutes of April 1796 as being at the north end of Gillingham Dam, the dam being the causeway upon which the road was constructed over the river's marshy flood plain.

Approaching Gillingham from this direction today, the toll-house was on the left at a cross-roads.

55

5.0 Appendix: The Impostors

Buildings in Suffolk that are not Toll-houses

When researching and looking for toll-houses in any county, one's first attempts will undoubtedly focus on various octagonal ended buildings near the roadside that seem to offer themselves up as likely candidates.

We have seen from the foregoing gazetteer that in Suffolk this type of toll-house, as found at Sicklesmere or Botesdale, is certainly not the norm. In fact the norm for the area appears to be the foursquare two storey house or single storey bungalow, usually with a central porch and the requisite side gable windows for vision up and down the road, such as those found at Claydon, Eye, Mildenhall Fen or Carlton.

In order to prevent the inevitable "but what about the toll-house at ....?" type questions that might follow the publication of this book, the following appendix includes a fair selection of octagonal ended buildings from around the county. It seems that many such buildings were built, mainly as lodges or cottages ornées. Thus the octagonal form is certainly not unknown in Suffolk as the following pages will testify, it is just that the toll-house builders chose not to use it for some reason.

These 'impostors' are presented in roughly the same order as the main gazetteer of toll-houses, i.e. from west to east across the county. Many of these are from parishes where a toll-house was expected to be found, and many of them have for varying lengths of time led the author slightly astray. It is hoped that diligent research has by now weeded out all such impostors from the gazetteer proper, so that they are all relegated to this appendix..

The author will of course be pleased to hear enquiries of the form "but what about the impostor at ....?", they almost warrant a book of their own!

London Lodge, Brandon
TL 769852

This interesting little lodge with its flint walls and red brick dressings around 'gothick' windows is about a quarter mile nearer the town than the former toll-house described on p.33.

It does indeed have an octagonal end, a central doorway and two side facing windows, but this all faces onto a driveway into Brandon Park, rather than the nearby main road.

It is therefore not a toll-house.

photo: polystar

Lodge, Elveden
TL 820798

One of several lodges of varying sizes to Elveden Hall, this one does unusually have a doorway facing the main road and a roof projecting over the door to provide some protection from the weather.

The side wings are octagonal ended, of red brick and tile construction, with added on elements of exposed timber framing and render, and thus belongs with the other lodges along this road.

The original toll-house here (p.32) was actually on the other side of the road.

photo: polystar

Round House, Denston
TL 765527

This small octagonal cottage near the village of Denston, south-west of Bury St Edmunds, sits in a very visible position at a road junction.

It is however not a toll-house, but a grade II listed lodge to the nearby Denston Hall.

Very much in the cottage ornée tradition it is rendered with an overhanging thatched roof carried on timber columns.

photo: polystar

The Lodge, Great Barton
TL 890669

Another flint lodge with red brick dressings, but here with square headed windows, with drip moulds over, and a thatched roof.

This hexagonal section of a larger building is quite prominent and faces a road junction in the centre of Great Barton. It has a blocked up doorway facing the adjacent lane, but is not however the long lost Barton Gate on the Scole to Bury St Edmunds road (see p.36).

photo: polystar

Round House, Rougham
TL 914646

This grade II listed round house is a former lodge to Rougham Hall on the Thurston road, which never was part of the turnpike network.

It is constructed of flint with white brick dressings, probably from nearby Woolpit.

Although screened by trees, it can be seen well in the winter months from the nearby railway line when coming out of Thurston station.

photo: polystar

Cattle Market Toll-house, Bury St Edmunds
TL 851643

This small octagonal building with a decorative slate roof on ornate eaves brackets and weatherboarded walls sits in a car park in Bury St Edmunds, awaiting redevelopment.

Whether it will survive is uncertain, its former use, presumably for collecting market tolls, now long redundant. One hope is that it might be resited somewhere to give it a new lease of life.

photo: polystar

Toll Cottage, Lavenham
TL 916493

Timber-framed and limewashed, this grade II listed 16th century building would have preceded the turnpikes by some two centuries.

It is however a genuine toll-house, one where market tolls were paid in the centre of Market Place, Lavenham, quite near the guildhall.

Probably the only such relatively intact survival in Suffolk, such 'toll-houses' can be found elsewhere in the country, as in the Cotwolds, where the adjoining market toll board was photographed.

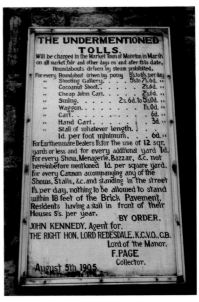

photo: polystar

photo: polystar

Lodge, Assington
TL 934394

Another grade II listed lodge, this one is timber-framed and rendered with a thatched roof. It is listed as late 18th or early 19th century, a lodge to Assington Hall, which burnt down in 1957.

South of Sudbury on the A134 Colchester road, it is set back in a lay-by where the road has been straightened. The strange thing is that it is on the opposite side of the road to Assington Park, within which the main house was presumably situated.

photo: polystar

Octagon Cottage, Hitcham
TL 993534

The name seems to say it all, but although octagonal ended, this brick and pantile cottage in Hitcham is unusual in its design, having a roof of only two slopes and a central ridge, rather than the more usual hipped end wrapping around.

The gable facing the road does appear to have had a doorway blocked up, but this is no toll-house, as the turnpike roads did not come this way.

photo: polystar

Horse Mill, Stowmarket
TM 050596

Just north of the town of Stowmarket, but not on the right road to be a toll-house, this small octagonal building could lead the unwary astray, especially since the Stowmarket toll-house proper is nowhere to be found (see p.40).

It is situated quite high above the nearby road, and is in fact a former horse mill on a farm, now converted into living accommodation.

photo: polystar

The Mustard Pot, Needham Market
TM 096548

Not really an impostor, this is the toll-house that used to stand by the A140 at Brockford, re-erected south-east of Needham Market, near the lake, but now well away from any main road (see p.42).

Due for demolition in the early 1970's because of proposed road widening, it was moved to its present site by Mr Jan Sniechowski, originally for use as a fishing lodge.

In the early 1980's it served as a house, and in 1986 was extended for its present use as a veterinary surgery.

photo: polystar

photo: stowe veterinary group

Railway Building, Mellis
TM 100746

Very much in the style of a more elaborate toll-house, this octagonal ended building, near the Railway Tavern, adjoins the level crossing in the village of Mellis, some way from the nearest turnpike road.

Presumably all in red brick, now painted, its crenellated parapet and 'gothick' doorway (albeit set within a classical doorcase) all hark back to the 'picturesque'.

photo: polystar

Railway Building, Eye Station
TM 143738

Another octagonal ended railway building, this one at Eye Station is not unlike the Mellis example, but lacks the crenellations and gothick doorway.

The railway terminus here was mainly for goods, the line branching off the Ipswich to Norwich main line some three miles to the west at Mellis.

photo: polystar

Tollgate House, Braiseworth
TM 114719

This curious roadside cottage between Brockford and Scole on the A140 is called 'Tollgate House' for no apparent reason. It does sit fairly close to the highway edge and could conceivably have served the purpose.

It appears to be of Victorian date, built at a time when the trusts were beginning to feel the pinch with the railways. The problem is that although this is a turnpike route, there is no record of a toll-house hereabouts, neither in turnpike records nor on old maps.

photo: polystar

Old Toll House, Debenham
TM 173634

This is not the Debenham toll-house associated with the turnpike road that ran past it, but another earlier toll-house for the collection of market tolls.

Timber-framed internally, but not so obviously ancient as the Lavenham example (p.63), this little building is now part of a terrace adjoining what was Debenham's former Market Place.

photo: polystar

Lodge, Witnesham
TM 183510

Although the two of these shown opposite are very near Swilland, all three of these lodges to Witnesham Hall are probably in Witnesham parish, as was the actual toll-house site the author had been seeking (see p.42).

These 'gothick' windowed early nineteenth century lodges are all quite similar, however subtle differences can be spotted in the windows, roofs and chimneys, some probably original, others due to later alterations.

photo: polystar

Lodges near Swilland
TM 183523 & 183525

photo: polystar

photo: polystar

Lodge to Crowe Hall, Stutton
TM 153346

This interesting stone built gate house with crenellated parapet and carved pinnacles is tucked well away from any turnpike roads in the south of the Shotley peninsula.

It serves as a gatehouse to Crowe Hall and was meant to impress, its fine ashlar work and refined gothick style windows indicative of no expense spared.

Essentially just a single ground floor room it has had to have a discreetly attached link to an extension to be of any use.

photo: polystar

Lodge, Bentley Park
TM 119382

This early Victorian lodge in red brick with white brick dressings is nowhere near a turnpike route.

However it does adjoin the route of a former railway line, the branch line off the Ipswich to Colchester mainline that formerly served the small town of Hadleigh.

This might explain its 'railway' architecture appearance, but not its octagonal shape.

photo: polystar

Lodge, Wherstead Park
TM 157407

Again nowhere near a turnpike route, but borrowing the toll-house design ethic, this lodge stands at the entrance to the big house at Wherstead Park, just south of Ipswich.

Now part of the local electricity company's estate there, it is built in the local 'Suffolk White' brick to match the house and has a decorative fish-scale slate roof.

photo: polystar

Round House, Belstead
TM 133412

This grade II listed round house is described as an early 19th century lodge, but to which estate is totally unclear. It is to be found near the centre of the village of Belstead, south-west of Ipswich.

It is certainly not on any known turnpike route, but with its 'gothick' windows and two storey octagonal core with side wings, it could easily be mistaken for a toll-house elsewhere in the country.

photo: polystar

Round House, Walton
TM 290360

On the Ipswich side of Felixstowe's outskirts, this is where there would have been a toll-house, had this road been turnpiked.

This hexagonal building appears to be timber-framed and rendered. It has a brick plinth and 'gothick' windows with good visibility up and down the road.

The 1881 first edition 25" Ordnance Survey map has it clearly shown as 'Round House'.

photo: polystar

Round House, Thorington
TM 434736

Up the A12 just north of Yoxford and rather too close to the Blythburgh toll-house to be any use to the turnpike road, this thatched flint and brick cottage ornée is listed grade II and currently used as a restaurant.

It is sited where a lane from Thorington village joins the main road and was probably the north-eastern lodge to the now demolished Thorington Hall.

photo: polystar

Rookery Lodge, Yoxford
TM 398687

These three single storey octagonal ended lodges serve as gatehouses to two of the three large estates that surround Yoxford: two are on the northern approaches either side of the A12 and one is in the centre of the village.

Interestingly they demonstrate between them virtually the entire palette of Suffolk's vernacular building materials. The eastern lodge to Cockfield Hall is rendered and thatched, Rookery Lodge nearly opposite is in 'Suffolk White' brick with a slate roof, whilst the southern lodges to Cockfield Hall in The Street are a pair in soft 'Suffolk Red' brick with interesting crow-stepped gables.

Another lodge with weather-boarding and a clay tiled roof would complete the set.

photo: polystar

Lodges to Cockfield Hall, Yoxford
TM 394690 & 399691

photo: polystar

photo: polystar

Abbey Cottage, Theberton
TM 449643

This grade II listed building is described in Leiston's Official Guide as a toll cottage, which it certainly is not. It does not actually adjoin the road from Aldeburgh to Middleton, but sits off it on a side road that leads to Eastbridge.

It was probably a lodge to nearby Leiston Old Abbey and is hexagonal in plan, built of flint and brick with a thatched roof and 'gothick' windows.

About half a mile north of here can be found 'The Roundhouse', which is semi-detached, not so round and not a toll-house either.

photo: polystar

6.0 Bibliography

Albert, W. 1972 *Turnpike Road System in England 1663-1840* Cambridge

Alderton, D. & Booker, J. 1980 *The Industrial Archaeology of East Anglia* Batsford

Chatwin, C.P. 1961 *East Anglia and Adjoining Areas* British Regional Geology HMSO

Clifford, S. & King, A. (eds) 1993 *Local Distinctiveness* Common Ground

Cossons, A. 1951 *The Turnpike Roads of Norfolk* Norfolk and Norwich Archaeological Society vol.XXX part III

Cruickshank, D. & Wyld, P. 1975 *London: The Art of Georgian Building* Architectural Press

Dymond, D. & Martin, E. (eds) 1999 *An Historical Atlas of Suffolk* Suffolk County Council / Suffolk Institute of Archaeology & History

Freethy, R. 1987 *Turnpikes and Toll Houses of Lancashire* Countryside

Harris, R. (ed) (no date) *Weald & Downland Open Air Museum Guidebook*

Kanefsky, J. 1976 *Devon Tollhouses* Exeter Industrial Archaeology Group

Mogg, E. 1829 *Paterson's Roads* London

Mowl, T. & Earnshaw, B. 1985 *Trumpet at a Distant Gate* Waterstone

Pawson, E. 1977 *Transport and Economy: The Turnpike Roads of Eighteenth Century Britain* Academic Press

Searle, M. 1930 *Turnpikes and Toll-Bars* Hutchinson

Serjeant, W.R. & Penrose, D.G. (eds) 1973 *Suffolk Turnpikes* E Suffolk RO

Sexton, L. 2008 *Fifty Four Miles to Yarmouth* Dunnock Books

Smith, P. 1970 *The Turnpike Age* Luton Museum and Art Gallery

Wright, G.N. 1992 *Turnpike Roads* Shire

Of Related Interest:

The Toll-houses of Cornwall

Patrick Taylor   2001   £7.95
ISBN 0 902660 29 2   iv+80pp
Federation of Old Cornwall Societies

Companion volume to the present one, contains a similar introductory essay and history of the turnpike roads in Cornwall, followed by an extensive gazetteer of toll-houses and their former sites.

"A useful detailed county study with photographs of high quality" *Industrial Archaeology Review*

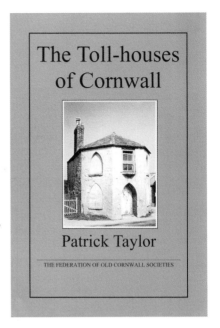

The Toll-houses of Norfolk

Patrick Taylor   2009   £7.95
ISBN 978 1 907154 02 7   iv+76pp
Polystar Press

Research interrupted by the Norwich Library fire finally resumed and brought to publication.

Essentially the same format as this Suffolk volume: history of the turnpike roads, detailed gazetteer of the county plus an appendix on the impostors.

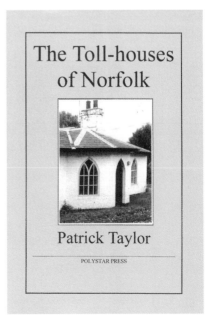